The Path Of The Mystic

By the same author

Spiritual Man in a New Age (DLT 1980)

THE PATH OF THE MYSTIC

Steps in a pilgrim's progress
with seven meditational exercises
Suitable for use by groups or individuals

PETER SPINK

Darton, Longman and Todd
London

First published in 1983 by
Darton, Longman and Todd Ltd
89 Lillie Road, London SW6 1UD

© Peter Spink 1983

ISBN 0 232 51563 8

British Library Cataloguing in Publication Data

Spink, Peter
  The path of the mystic.
  1. Meditation
  I. Title
  248.3   BV4813

ISBN 0–232–51563–8

Phototypeset by Input Typesetting Ltd, London SW19 8DR
Printed in Great Britain by the Anchor Press Ltd
and bound by Wm Brendon & Son Ltd
both of Tiptree, Essex.

With gratitude to Ludi
who pointed the way

No man can reveal to you aught but that which already lies asleep in the dawning of your knowledge. If he is indeed wise he does not bid you enter the house of his wisdom but rather leads you to the threshold of your own mind.

The Prophet
Kahil Gibran

Contents

Introduction

'There are too many merchants of theory. The time has come to see, to do, and to understand.' (L. Pattel, *Gurdjieff*. Times Press, New York, 1964) If these are the characteristics of an awakened man, then they are also the indications of a valid mysticism. For the path of the true mystic is but the straight path of what F. C. Happold calls 'experimental wisdom'. It is concerned with seeing, doing and understanding.

'The Path of the Mystic' is not therefore a book about mysticism or a study of its classical forms. Its concern is what it describes as the business of living, for this is the *raison d'être* of experimental wisdom.

Nevertheless the path of the mystic is not at variance with those forms and structures within which Western mysticism has traditionally expressed itself. It resonates completely with orthodoxy of belief, and experiences no difficulty with the definitions of Christian theology. Indeed its concern is with the essence of doctrine and dogma. This could not be otherwise, for truth in its dual manifestation of dynamic and cult, i.e. experimental wisdom and intellectual concepts, cannot be at variance with itself. The former's concern is that of understanding at a level other than thought, the latter's sphere is that of the intellect. Yet the way of experimental wisdom cannot properly be judged by a set of intellectual propositions, for this would be to encapsulate God who alone is truly orthodox.

'By their fruits', said Jesus, 'ye shall know them.' This is the perspective taken in this book. It uses no other criteria for determining the nature of the path and the direction it takes.

In his book *The Teaching of the Mystics* (Mentor Books 1960) Walter T. Stace describes the diversity of forms within which a valid mysticism can manifest.

> Mysticism naturally, though not necessarily, becomes intimately associated with whatever is the religion of the culture in which it appears . . . . Mystical experience in itself does not have any tendency to make a man a Christian or a Buddhist. Into the framework of what creed he will fit his experience will tend to depend mostly on the culture in which he lives. If he is a highly sophisticated modern individual who has been turned by his education into a religious sceptic he may remain a sceptic as regards the dogmas of the different religions, but he is likely at the same time to feel that in that experience he has found something sacred.

It is this principle, that mysticism is the essence manifesting in diversity of form, which has governed the use of language in this book. It uses no technical or specialist vocabulary. Words are but the dress in which experimental wisdom is clothed. Such clothing may be taken up or discarded as occasion requires. Its dress may be religious or secular, and frequent changes may be both desirable and necessary. A security which is invested in language is a false one, and a religious experience irretrievably wedded to a particular terminology is divorced from reality. The 'eternal verities' traditionally expressed in such specifically religious language as salvation, grace and sin are essential elements of the straight path, but over-familiarity with such words has, for vast numbers of people who are totally committed to the Way, denuded them of all significance.

In times of rapid social change such as those in which we live today, the transmission of ideas is likely to require diversity of thought-forms. The intermingling of cultures, especially those of East and West, precludes rigidity of language. All verbal communication is incomplete and no one vocabulary can adequately express for all men the reality it is intended to signify.

There is also the constant danger of identifying outward form with inner reality, and equating the adoption of a particular vocabulary with that which it does but signify. This particular difficulty is accentuated by the direction in which Western education has been traditionally weighted. For education has been equated with the cultivation of the intellect. In the pursuit of this the faculty of imagination has been neglected and that of the intuition ignored. The result of this is that the cultivation of perception has been reduced to seeing with the eye and hearing with the ear.

No one exclusive title is given in the book to the followers of experimental wisdom. The terms pilgrim, mystic, people of the Way and contemplatives are used interchangeably. He who has uncovered within himself the still centre is centred in the heart. He is therefore Christ-centred. It is in meeting the demands of the straight path that we acquire the right to that title which Jesus conferred upon his immediate followers, i.e. 'my disciples'.

Parallel to the upheavals which Western society is now experiencing is a great search for guidelines which will, in the absence of the old and familiar landmarks provided by external restraints and authorities, give a clear sense of direction. This search transcends all the old barriers created by belief-patterns and thought-forms. Dogmatic consciousness is rapidly disappearing, yet in a world of disintegration and impermanence there is everywhere discernible an intense desire to discover and relate to objective reality.

The mystical path is concerned with this reality, i.e. the life impulse in all creation. This impulse or movement may be seen as the 'dynamic'. It operates within individuals and communities. It is the evolutionary impulse which, at times of crisis and change within the human race, indicates the direction humanity must take if it is to survive.

The aims of this book are twofold: to indicate first of all the landmarks by which the straight path may be recognized and, secondly, the means by which its dynamic may be uncovered. The first is followed in the form of a pilgrimage, the second by a series of meditational exercises.

It is often assumed that to study the words of Scripture leads inevitably to increase of perception and the uncovering of the dynamic. The reverse is frequently the case. The process of analysis set in motion by such study leads invariably into culs de sac of profitless speculation. The assumption that assimilation of mental concepts leads straight to an unveiling of the dynamic is a fallacy. This error has long been reinforced in the minds of multitudes of 'believers' by the imbalance of educational methods, both religious and secular. All sacred Scripture does indeed have a special function in relation to the dynamic. For the Scriptures *par excellence* both articulate and confirm this. Yet there is nothing automatic or magic about the process. Understanding is a prerequisite for their proper usage.

Without prior cultivation of the capacity to relate to the spirit rather than the letter of the Scriptures, Bible reading and listening rapidly becomes self-defeating. Economy of usage and the reverential awareness which springs from a conscious cultivation of the still centre make it possible to penetrate beyond the mere sound of words. When imagination and intuition are also brought into operation, the component parts of Scripture form a whole. This is true contemplation.

The Bible passages for use in the meditations at the end of each chapter do not precede but follow the meditational exercises, i.e. the finding of the still centre. The passage then becomes a mirror image of that which has already been touched in the stillness. The Scriptures do the work of reflecting awareness back, not into analysis or introspection, but to that point of consciousness where the dynamic is struggling to manifest. So do they speak as the Word of God, and confirm the straightness of the path and the traveller in the Way.

1

The How of Learning

The initial step, the first lesson to be learned as we set out on the path of experimental wisdom, is the 'how of learning'.

For a long time in the Western world there has been a strong tendency to equate education both secular and religious with the grasping of ideas by the intellect. The gain, if such it can be called, from this concept of education is that the so-called educated, the ones who are supposed to know, are in effect continually expanding encyclopaedias. The loss, and it is a heavy one, is that the information acquired is all too often totally divorced from the business of living.

This concept of study is pinpointed in the schoolboy story of the two children playing noisily in the presence of their grandmother, who was endeavouring to study her Bible. 'Hush!' said one to the other. 'Grandma is reading for her finals.'

The path upon which we are about to embark is concerned above all else with the business of living. Progress is evidenced by the development of a true self-awareness, an ability to relate to others and a capacity to see meaning and purpose in the world of which we are part. In other words it is a progressive recognition of that which we discover to be our true potential.

To effect this involves something other than the acquisition of theoretically useful information. It is the antithesis of seeking to store up knowledge against the future. Indeed the very cornerstone of the 'how of learning' is a recognition that intellectual acquisitiveness, the collecting of ideas, or the mental assent to ideals, far from effecting awakening and promoting growth, frequently block the capacity for understanding and response.

The beginning of learning therefore is an acknowledgement that, divorced from a response on a level other than the intellect, the amassing of information creates barriers against true learning. It is to know that definitions and concepts, however excellent, if unrelated to what in the context of this path is the primary level of perception, amount to the adding of no more than interesting – albeit 'spiritual' – supplements to existing encyclopaedias.

Such learning does not come easily, for the focusing of our attention upon something other than the grasping of ideas by the intellect involves cutting across deeply ingrained habits. It means the conscious and progressive disruption of long-established thought patterns and the recognition and control of automatic responses.

To attempt to do this outside the practice of disciplines directed towards this end invariably results in no more than the substitution of new thoughts for old, with consciousness still focused upon the acquisition of ideas, even though such ideas are about the necessity for a change of consciousness!

St Bernard, when asked the question: 'What is God?' replied: 'He is the one before whom all worlds recoil, ungraspable by the human intellect.' St Augustine wrote: 'There is in the mind of man no knowledge of God except that it does not know Him.'

Where then within man lies the faculty for this knowledge? And what is this primary level of perception?

The question and all its implications are answered with great clarity and simplicity in the book *Mr God This Is Anna* by Fynn (Collins, 1974, p. 83). The child Anna in conversation with Fynn describes it as follows:

> You know Mister God in my middle in your middle and everything you know, every person you know you know in your middle. Every person and everything you know has got Mister God in their middle, and so you have got their Mister God in your middle too.

To the childlike mind unconditioned by the years and untrammelled by imposed thought patterns it is, as Anna concluded, decisively 'easy'. For those commonly called mature and educated, even the religious, such perception lies at best dormant and at worst submerged beneath superstructures of so-called education. Hence the oft-repeated scriptural injunction to 'awaken' and to develop eyes to see and ears to hear.

It was for the awakening of this capacity to know as Anna describes it 'from one's middle' that St Paul said that he prayed for the readers of one of his letters. He expressed it as follows: 'I pray that the eyes of your heart may be opened that you may know . . . '

Here then lies the key to the 'how of learning'. This is the capacity towards which our attention must be directed and again and again redirected if we are to find and continue along the path of experimental wisdom. This alone will determine whether the path we follow is one of true education or of indoctrination. For whilst the former enables us to become partakers of that truth which Jesus declares sets men free, the latter imposes burdens grievous to be borne. And here lies the great irony that in the name of 'good news' man's capacity to hear is thus effectively silenced!

Implicit in the question of the 'how of learning' is a second question. It is this. 'How is consciousness thus directed and focused?' or 'How is the process of true learning initiated?' (To this we shall come in the exercise given at the end of this chapter.) For the answer can never be given in the abstract, but only in the practice of those disciplines which so focus the consciousness, or in what Jesus called the doing of the truth.

It is here at the very beginning of the journey, even as he contemplates the first step along the way, that the pilgrim is confronted with the possibility of departing from the path. This takes place with the descent of the great Cloud of Delusion. The descent of this cloud is rapid, and so quickly does it engulf and wrap itself around the pilgrim that he fails to observe what is happening (i.e. that he is in fact departing from the path). His faculty for self-observation is not yet fully functioning. So how can he know? It is this cloud which again and again at every stage of the journey, like a great fog, envelops the people on the way and effects a speedy departure from the path. What is this delusion? It is the substitution of knowing about for knowing. The results of the digression are both insidious and immediate. The thirst for information is now directed to something new. The old-established pattern of the grasping intellect reasserts itself and a study of that very faculty by which true knowledge is acquired now takes place. The focus of attention has changed. There is a radical shift of interest, but it still proceeds from the same source – the acquisitive intellect. What is still to be recognized is that to acknowledge the need for direct perception is still not to perceive.

So does the pilgrim depart swiftly and easily from the straight path. He has now acquired a new and frequently absorbing preoccupation which may easily and rapidly become an obsession. He is concerned with studying the theory of direct perception and the necessity for knowledge, indeed, the 'how of learning'.

The pilgrim has now changed direction and before him looms the Maze of Fascination. A panorama of new perspectives bursts upon his vision. They range from the religious to the psychological – the radical to the traditional. The claims and counterclaims of many and varied traditions sweep into his consciousness. Two factors are common to all. First, each alternative path in this maze of fascination presents rationales, thought-forms, terms of reference and study patterns for that which the pilgrim still does not know and from which he remains blocked off. They constitute areas for fascinating research. The path he is now following is one of the pursuit of knowledge.

The second factor which they have in common is that all converge to one point – in the direction of a library of encyclopaedic knowledge, a vast storehouse of information. So is the path of true learning left behind and superseded by the process of 'ever learning and never coming to a knowledge of the truth'.

As the pilgrim moves along this way the cloud of delusion expands into a dreamlike fog of thoughts which breed more and more thought-forms, and these in turn create culs-de-sac of sterile knowledge.

The journey has now become – albeit unconsciously – one of thought and fantasy. The pilgrimage has ended before it began. But this the pilgrim will not know. For in his dreamlike state thought has expanded into intensive study. And the fruit of such is the birth of strong convictions. These convictions he will elevate into fundamentals of the faith to be communicated with fervour to all who (themselves not having learned to know from their middles as Anna so accurately described it), will, in like manner receive 'the truth'. They in turn 'communicate'. Sadly such communications are frequently called 'witnessing to the truth' – even truth about the opening of the eyes of the heart!

During the late forties and early fifties, young missionaries arriving in India for the first time found themselves involved in the then very topical debate concerning the learning of languages. New recruits were being thrown in at the deep end as it were, and without prior grammatical preparation plunged into situations where learning came through using the language. This deep-end experience was seen as comparable to the process whereby a child learns. The process was sometimes painful, for it involved the cutting across of pre-conceived notions and expectancy. It was known as the direct method.

In the path of experimental wisdom it is the direct method alone which can awaken the faculty for knowledge, effect entrance into the path and facilitate progress. There is no alternative. 'For', said Jesus, 'except you become as little children you shall in no wise enter' . . .

If the journey for which we are now preparing ourselves

is to be more than one of thought, fantasy and ultimately self-delusion, then it is the direct method to which we must commit ourselves. What is this method? It is first of all a conscious directing of the will towards a clearly defined purpose. There can be no ambiguity concerning our aims, the point of departure or the path into which it leads. To each one of these Jesus addressed himself unequivocally. The goal he described as the pearl of great price, or life with an eternal quality. The attainment of the goal is only by the selling of all that one possesses or the turning away from all false values. The point of departure or entry on to the path he declared to be through a strait gate or a pure heart – that is one with unclouded vision. The nature of the path was, he said, narrow. To this he added the words 'and few there be that find it'.

We need then to look carefully at the effecting of an entrance through the strait gate. Our concern is to enter, not to speculate or formulate theories as to how. For speculation leads immediately into the diversions we have described.

St Paul, as we have already noted, gives us a clear guideline which leads immediately to the point of beginning. It runs directly parallel to the guideline given by Jesus in answer to speculation concerning the Kingdom of God. Both lead to something 'within'. The words of Jesus describe entrance, Paul speaks of vision. They point to one and the same reality.

And it is at this point that we ourselves may test the guidelines. For they direct us not to concepts or ideas apart from ourselves, not primarily to belief structures, but to the heart of our being. And lest we should be tempted here to raise the objection that this is introspection and subjective, let us note at once that we are directed to a point of consciousness beyond intellect and emotion. This we shall examine carefully later.

The methods of Jesus and Paul are identical. Both throw us directly back upon ourselves, not haphazardly but with clear and unmistakable guidance. When the guideline is thus followed – that is when place, space and cognizance are given to this level of perception – a powerful resonance is made between that which until now has lain buried below the level of consciousness and the truth enshrined in the words of Scripture. The word of God is heard, deep calls to deep and like to like, and for the first time the pilgrim hears; this hearing is also a true seeing.

What is this seeing? And how may it be achieved? Clearly this is a perception quite different and distinct from the function of the physical eye.

The eyes of the head are linked to the perception of externals. Those of the heart have a capacity for vision which penetrates the veils created by physical form and manifestation. To look from this source is consciously to take a new perspective. It is the deliberate focusing of a faculty which enables insight attainable in no other way. As we have seen, such observation may be described both as a seeing and a knowing. And to the one who is thus learning to see and to know, an infinity of vistas begins to unfold. It is the beginning of knowing reality or truth and a seeing of God.

Many generations of children have been entranced by the story of the sleeping princess. Like the parables of Jesus it is a beautiful and fascinating story. For those who have eyes to see and ears to hear it is much more than a delightful fairy tale. It embodies an ageless wisdom and a universal truth which, to use the language of St Paul, is for 'those who are ripe for it'. Again, like the parables of Jesus, it is both for children and the childlike who, said Jesus, are the ones who 'enter the Kingdom'.

At the heart of the fortress lies the highly desirable and beautiful princess, surrounded and enclosed by the all-but impenetrable thickets. Only the prince's sword can cut a way through. There at the very centre the princess is awakened by a kiss. Here then is an earthly story with a heavenly meaning. It is indeed a parable of the Kingdom. For the penetration of the thicket is the prerogative of the inheritor of a kingdom.

He who will penetrate the innermost centre where true union is to be effected must first penetrate the barriers. And it is these barriers which we face and through which we must effect an entrance if we are to effect entrance into the way, the truth and the life.

Browning in his *Paracelsus* gives us a word picture of the same truth:

> There is an inmost centre in us all
> Where Truth abides in fullness: and around
> Wall upon wall, the gross flesh hems it in,
> That perfect clear perception – which is truth.
> A baffling and perverting carnal mesh
> Binds it, and makes all error: and to KNOW*
> Rather consists in opening out a way
> Whence the imprisoned splendour may escape,
> Then in effecting entry for a light
> Supposed to be without.

*author's capitals

The gross flesh describes with some poetic licence the barriers to be penetrated. They are physical, emotional and intellectual, aspects of man which, when uncontrolled and turbulent, shroud consciousness and powerfully inhibit that 'perfect clear perception'.

The basis of all our meditational exercises then is the stilling of that perpetual motion. This alone can effect a proper relationship between body, mind and emotions, a restoration of a balance which makes entrance possible.

MEDITATIONAL EXERCISE

1 Basic Exercise as in the Appendix

2 In imagination build up around you a picture of peace and tranquillity. For example you may see yourself as sitting alone by the seashore, or in the countryside. All around you is space. This space breathes stillness and calm. Allow yourself to relax into the scene. Let its stillness penetrate your being and become yours even as you respond to it from the still centre within yourself.

3 Silence

4 Closing sentence:
   In him was life and the life was the light of men.

5 Reading:
   Then the disciples came and said to him, 'Why do you speak to them in parables?' And he answered them, 'To you it has been given to know the secrets of the kingdom of heaven, but to them it has not been given. For to him who has will more be given, and he will have abundance,

but from him who has not, even what he has will be taken away.'

Matthew 13:10–13

6 Invocation: as in Appendix

2

Intuitive Knowledge

Finding the inmost centre is a discipline. But we should divest the word of any false meaning or overtone. What we have described as a discipline and put into effect through our meditational exercise is the clearing away of debris, the creating of a point of access, and the creation of an observation platform. And in this threefold activity there is no element of repression or restrictive practice. Rather is this the creation of space, from which things as they are may be observed.

What is the nature and effect of this process and how does it relate to the birth of intuitive insight? It is of its very essence that it should operate with complete detachment. For without this it is impossible to see and the vision is immediately clouded. Emotional involvement leads at once to identification with aspects of that which is being observed. When this happens there can be no cognition of things as they really are, for this prevents a seeing of the whole.

Although the development of intuition can neither be understood nor explained by the intellect there is nothing haphazard, unplanned nor uncontrolled in its development. Stage by stage it unfolds as the pilgrim persists in practising the disciplines which create the conditions necessary for its growth. It begins with the flowering of true self-observation – a regarding of oneself divested of any element of emotional involvement. Operating from a point of complete detachment, it is quite distinct from introspection.

From this fundamental first step springs the growth of an accurate perception of other people. This also is without emotional involvement, which again by its very nature produces entanglement with the object of observation and precludes clarity of vision. This perception is a capacity to see through those veils with which all human beings are surrounded and which constitute the *persona* or mask which hides reality. These veils are the assumed and imposed behaviour patterns; barriers erected against intrusion and for the protection of that self or ego, which as we shall see, must give way before the true and universal self. They are the projected images, invariably divorced from reality, which form the basis of most human relationships and upon which the frameworks of society are based. These hide the hidden splendour and are the 'gross flesh' of Browning's *Paracelsus*.

Characteristic of this perception is its absence of intrusion or judgement, and this for a very clear reason. The nature of its seeing is a recognition of that potential for spiritual unfolding which exists at the heart of all men. It therefore evokes respect and hope in the one who sees.

Perception of people, is by its very nature, linked to insight into contemporary society. The pilgrim is therefore part of a paradox. He is both completely detached from, yet totally involved with, the world of people as it exists in his day. As we have seen, this detachment, not only from individuals but from society, enables him to observe potential, and this potential contains all the elements of meaning and purpose which he sees to be part of an unfolding purpose for all mankind. This comprehension of the world of people in its turn focuses his perceptions into the great movements of history which shape the destiny of man. Indeed there is nothing which eludes this true seeing. It is part of a breath-taking opening up of vast horizons involving the whole of life, giving insight into an understanding of the past, present and future. And all this lies within each of those who will practise those disciplines which make possible the discovery of the still centre.

The journey then has truly begun. Consciousness is now being trained to centre in the place of 'perfect clear perception'. The former tyranny of the intellect is now giving way to a right relationship between the faculty for direct knowledge and that of thought processes. A new awareness is coming to birth. A school of learning has been entered. The way ahead abounds in promise. There is no limit to the possibilities which are now appearing on the horizon. But it is here at this point of realization that the pilgrim may lose his way, that a change of direction may easily take place. Indeed it is the very intensity of his realization of potential and opportunity which may determine this change. For such a realization may effect for the unwary a rapid but unrecognized shift of consciousness from the still centre to the emotions – emotions which now identify with the vision first seen from the still centre. Space and detachment give place to emotional involvement which now takes control. Objectivity is lost, for the flood of emotion sweeps away all clarity of vision. Perspective changes, and the straight path ahead disappears from the pilgrim's line of vision. Will and emotions now combine to create new vistas. The imagination is brought into play and personal desire begins to project its own images. At the very place of discovery the pilgrim now plunges headlong into the Mirage of Glamour. The ego or lower self has full reign.

All desert dwellers are familiar with that creation of the feverish and uncontrolled imagination, the phenomenon called the mirage. To the traveller in the desert who is conscious only of intense desire, the mirage appears on the horizon as an image of the very thing which is desired. It is a projection of the imagination, a tantalizing hallucination without substance and, like the rainbow, the space between it and the viewer cannot be bridged. So are the conditions for self-deception established and perpetuated for the pilgrim in the way. When desire becomes the motivating factor, he inevitably becomes subject to self-deception. Because of this said Jesus again and again, 'Watch'. For this there can be no substitute.

Let us look at the characteristics of this mirage which deceives and eventually destroys the vision of those who become emotionally centred. It constitutes a kaleidoscopic vision of swiftly changing images. For when consciousness is centred in the emotions there can be no constancy. The mirage consists of a powerful vortex of forces having their origin, not within the heart or true centre of man, but from another centre which, when the intuitive faculty is out of operation, is quickly confused with the still centre. In current and common parlance it is the place of 'gut reaction'. Let us be quite clear about this; it is not the heart. It is far removed both from the place of clear perception and detachment. It is the place of emotional involvement, frequently confused with love. The mirage is but a projection of the uncontrolled emotions which emanate from this centre.

The pilgrim who is so entrapped from now on finds himself tossed to and fro within the whole range of human emotions. His awareness is now the prisoner of capricious and fluctuating feelings. Self-observation is replaced by its great counterfeit introspection, and he is caught up within the conflict of rapidly changing and competing feelings which impede all progress. Paradoxically he may for a time have the illusion of rapid progress along the path, though this imagined progress quickly gives way to confusion of aims and eventually to hopelessness.

Having moved from the place of stability and clear perception (i.e. from his true centre), the pilgrim is now disorientated and begins to search frantically for landmarks which will give a clear sense of direction. Introspection may now give birth to frequent bouts of self-denigration and its inevitable corollary, a judgemental attitude to others. All that is negative within his personality, in others and in society, will predominate in his consciousness. In desperation he will search for an escape. This 'search' will, in the absence of the authentic guidelines, lead eventually in one of two directions: either into culs-de-sac of imposed authority or the world of psychic illusion.

Authoritarian systems of great variety, but having in common the offer of absolute security in return for intellectual and emotional submission, will proffer instant solutions to the pilgrim's dilemma. Such capitulation will exact its toll in terms of an effective closing off from the still centre, with the substitution of deposits of 'truth' for 'knowledge of the truth' which, says Jesus, sets men free.

Alternatively, in the absence of competing authoritarian systems, the pilgrim may be plunged further into introspection. In his bedazzled state he may continue to experience the illusion of seeing, for, centred in his own emotions, he will find rapport with the whole world of emotions which surround and emanate from people, places and events. There will be a kind of knowing which is the calling of like to like. But this knowing will operate within the strict limits of the world of emotions. It will know nothing of the causes which produce emotional states, for it perceives only the effects of such causes. This is the world of psychic illusion.

The pull of this world is very powerful and it contains great and varying attractions. It is therefore important that the pilgrim should at this stage take note of it. As indicated, it is the great counterfeit to the world of reality. Its names are legion, for its appearance is constantly changing according to the desires of those who create it. Its appearance may be both religious and secular, for the pilgrim is now creating a world of his own which has no reality other than that which he gives to it. It has, however, two fixed characteristics by which it may always be recognized if viewed from the observer platform. Its fundamental appeal is always to the emotions and its effect is to swamp judgement and vision. For the pilgrim who is thus enmeshed there is but one way of escape. It is to return to the centre, the place where discernment and true objectivity may be established. The mirage of glamour can be dispelled by no other means. He must take once more those steps he has already learned and in doing this he will discover a secret. This is a secret hidden and preserved at the point of his true beginning. It can be uncovered only as he returns to it again, as he retraces his steps to the still centre. And this is the secret, that the art of discernment is learned from the act of centring.

We can now look a little more closely at the relation of intuition to intellect. For the pilgrim is now able to recognize that the mind is not to be equated with intellect or the activity of the brain, and that it encompasses much more than logical thinking or deductive reasoning. He is now aware of the capacity for what may be described as two kinds of thought, that is, penetrative and linear. The former is that of direct perception or intuitive awareness, the second is that of the logical or reasoning process. The first may be seen to relate to the heart, the second to the brain.

These two modes of perception are associated with two distinct kinds of meditation. Linear thought is that which operates in the context of reflective meditation – when the meditator is thinking about the object of his meditation. Penetrative thought is the act of becoming aware of, or contemplating, the significance of the whole. It is important that the relationship of these two methods of thought and their distinct modes of operation should be clearly seen. For the pilgrim who is pursuing a straight path and whose perspectives are fixed from the still centre, there is no ambiguity here. Penetrative thought precedes linear thinking in the pilgrim's progress. Intuitive awareness is the basis for intellectual activity or thinking. Contemplation prepares the way for reflection. In other words the picture must be fully seen before its worth can be explained. So the discipline of direct perception must first be cultivated and when this is done, the pilgrim discovers yet another secret. He finds that his capacity for linear thought, logical deduction, reflection and intellectual pursuit has increased beyond all expectation. He discovers that to restore the proper relationship of intuition and intellect is not to negate, but rather to increase, the capacity of the brain. Indeed this may be described as the restoration of a balance of these two aspects which when working together form what St Paul calls the 'mind of Christ'.

It is now possible to look at another aspect of the capacity for direct perception – that is the element of silence. As we have seen, the discipline basic to meditation is that of penetrating through the barriers of uncontrolled intellect and emotion to the centre or heart of our being. This heart is truly called the 'still' centre for it is a place of silence. It is in this silence that the pilgrim learns the art of direct perception or contemplation. Here he builds what is in effect a still clear pool of reflection. It is a mirror of reality, a silence which in turn gives birth to stillness and it is from stillness that accurate perception proceeds.

Here we have a picture which speaks directly to the imagination – the surface of a lake, untroubled by the movement of air, perfectly still beneath a cloudless sky. Such is the state of mind which mirrors reality. It is this balanced and fully developed mind which is created and reaffirmed through the practice of meditation and which the pilgrim learns to carry into all circumstances and every aspect of life.

But with every possibility for advance is also the possibility of diversion and in the very process of establishing the still pool of reflection the pilgrim may find a pitfall hard by the path, the pitfall of fear. This possible pitfall is kept open and its capacity continually enlarged by the activity of the many who, themselves being unable to discern the pilgrim way, are preoccupied in building other pathways.

What is the nature of this fear which now threatens to engulf the pilgrim? It is a fear which springs from insecurity, the uncertainty felt by the child who for the first time is learning to stand and walk alone.

In the Hindu Scriptures, the Upanishads, is an oft-quoted prayer: 'From the unreal lead me to the real. From darkness lead me to the light. From death lead me to immortality.' This is the direction which all the people of the Way must take. To make progress along this path means inevitably the letting go of all that is unreal. The pilgrim is now leaving behind many of the old familiar props. But there is no cause for fear. He is truly 'growing up into Christ'.

MEDITATIONAL EXERCISE

1 Basic Exercise

2 As in the previous meditation, build up around you a picture of tranquillity and peace. Be aware of the Light as it fills the picture, and surrounds you. Allow this Light to permeate your whole being. It is healing. Let it become both your inbreathing and outbreathing, and hold yourself in stillness at its centre.

3 Silence

4 Closing sentence:
That was the true Light which lighteth every man that cometh into the world.

5 Reading:
Philip said to Him, 'Lord, show us the Father, and we shall be satisfied.' Jesus said to him, 'Have I been with you so long, and yet you do not know me, Philip? He who has seen me has seen the Father; how can you say, "Show us the Father"? Do you not believe that I am in the Father and the Father in me? . . . I do not speak on my own authority, but the Father who dwells in me does his works.'

John 14:8–10

6 Invocation

3

The God Within

The pilgrim is now learning, with a steadily increasing sense of direction, to relate to reality within himself. To this his Will is being consciously directed. In the light of this reality he is also learning to recognize and dispel the illusion and delusion which conspire to divert him from the straight path. The shifting sands of capricious emotions on the one hand, and tyrannical intellect on the other, are seen in their true light.

Through the regular practice of spacing himself from their unfettered movement, he discovers them to be counterfeits of that true foundation upon which he must build. Nor is he deceived when these usurpers assume a guise devotionally and theologically acceptable. Yet such discernment, proceeding as it does from the still centre, will be free of all judgemental attitudes towards others. What he observes in people and situations beyond himself, he will also recognize as reflecting the attitudes and behaviour patterns of which he himself is capable. So, step by step, as he pursues the straight course, the subjective and transitory give place to that objective reality of which he is becoming aware.

It is now possible to define more clearly the nature of this reality which is being unveiled to consciousness. It is a place of tremendous discovery constituting space, but not a vacuum; stillness, yet a source of unceasing activity. This is that, for which if we choose, we may use the word 'God'. I say 'may', for this is not essential and it is important for the sake of integrity that the pilgrim allows this understanding fully and unreservedly into his consciousness. Failure to do so will create and perpetuate false and painful barriers between fellow travellers in the Way who for reasons of heritage or choice, accidents of history or birth, do not so define this reality. Their knowledge is expressed in other thought-forms. The one reality to which all undoubtedly relate and with which they fully share, is expressed in rationales of great diversity. And here we find clear New Testament guidelines. 'Not everyone', says Jesus, 'who says to me, "Lord, Lord," shall enter the kingdom of heaven, but he who does the will of my Father who is in heaven.'

The journey to which the pilgrim has committed himself and the path now being followed is concerned with knowledge of God. Such knowledge may be expressed in many ways or indeed, as far as language is concerned, remain unexpressed. This knowledge, as we have already seen, comes not with acceptance of the concept of God or with fidelity to a particular vocabulary, but by response to that which the word signifies. This comes about through penetrating the veils which separate consciousness from the real presence, signified in the life and death of Jesus when, in the words of the writer of the Epistle to the Hebrews, 'He entered into the inner shrine a forerunner on our behalf'. The means by which men come to this 'entering in' are many and varied. The frameworks of faith which evoke the desire to enter in are diverse and many-splendoured. Their structures are born of a multitude of differing cultures, yet they are all in part greater than their cultural and human origins. For the divine dynamic of history, or the Christ who fills all things, is the impulse without which no man can find the Way, the Truth and the Life. So are guidelines found for the Journey Inward.

For the majority of men, in most matters it is clear that it is not the title or the label which determine the nature of a thing, but the thing itself. Indeed this is so self-evident that to invert the order is manifestly absurd. But to those whose guarantee of reality is vested in verbal conformity and verification, this is not so. These are they for whom, in the search for the Divine, the shadow has superseded the substance; who are capable of listening only with the outward ear. Therefore they hear nothing of significance. With such men there is no cognizance of the fact that there are those for whom the word 'God' is inadequate and unacceptable.

In his book *The Journey Inward* F. C. Happold writes as follows:

> For many in our age the very word has become not only meaningless but also, since it carries so many overtones, a definite hindrance. Indeed, there is in the Western world today a strong reaction amongst many serious seekers after truth against the word because of the images with which it is associated, images far removed from reality and which threaten limitations and restrictions.

It was said of a great Indian sage who in the first half of this century visited many European countries, that his greatness was at once revealed by his capacity to convey truth through many different frameworks. To men of widely differing religions and of none, he was a channel which men recognized and to which they quickly responded. He used a variety of vocabularies and, regardless of background, people understood him. Believer, agnostic and atheist – all heard in their own tongue. And this was possible because the truth which he conveyed proceeded directly from his being, and pointed men unequivocally in the direction of reality within themselves. This, irrespective of language, was the truth which he transmitted with such power – truth authenticated by the fruitfulness of his life. The nature of such fruitfulness we shall examine later.

For many years before setting forth round the world he had lived in seclusion. In the forests of India he had followed disciplines of the Journey Inward. So had he learned to touch and find union with objective reality within himself, and it was this which he transmitted to others.

Not only has the word 'God' become devalued in our age but, as J. G. Phillips writes in *Your God is too Small*, for many it has become synonymous with beings of human creation. 'Many', he wrote:

> have captivated and found and trained to their own liking, something really far too big ever to be forced into little man-made boxes with neat little labels upon them. What is important is that we should learn to penetrate the reality which the word God signifies.

However, it is in the doing of this very thing that the pilgrim may well encounter a formidable barrier. Here, in the place of discernment, he faces what frequently appears as a serious hindrance to progress. It is the Wall of Confusion. The proportions and size of this wall are all the more clearly delineated by the light now unfolding within. For the nature of this light is wisdom, and in the presence of this, ignorance cannot flourish.

This powerful obstacle with which he is now confronted is created by the efforts of a great multitude of builders whose labours are unceasing. These are they, who by their most strenuous efforts would deny right of progress to all those People of the Way whose images of the Deity fail to conform to their own. Their right of way therefore, is not recognized.

Here there is confusion indeed, for although united in their desire and common effort to prevent by all means at their disposal the passage of all such nonconformists, the builders of the wall are also at variance with one another. Each vies with his neighbour and claims sole rights for building the wall. Such rights he insists, were delivered to his ancestors. The versatility of all the builders in the written laws and traditions which make for excellence in wall-building is beyond question. Their faculty in applying them reveals great skill, and in the art of wall-construction they are the undoubted masters. These are professionals whose special and exclusive communities have existed from time immemorial. They are in direct descent from those very experts to whom Jesus said: 'Woe to you, because you shut the kingdom of heaven against man'.

Daunting as the wall initially seems to the pilgrim, and indestructible as at first sight its substance appears, if he refuses to depart from the Path he cannot be hindered.

The perspective, if constantly renewed, will give him true insight into the situation. Observing from the still centre, he need not be deceived by outward appearances. Maintaining this perspective may not however be easy, for the conditioning which is the result of supposed education dies hard, and this may tempt him to meet the claims of the builders with counter-claims. In doing so he will quickly find himself contributing to the strength of this Wall! He too, will be a builder.

The builders will frequently be vociferous in their condemnation of those whose credentials they do not recognize. Quoting with great fervour from their sources of authority, they will spell out in detail the letter of their laws. The criteria by which the traveller pursues his pilgrimage will be questioned and derided; the disciplines from which he draws his strength dismissed as ineffectual. For, judging by the sight of their eyes and hearing only with their outward ears, they will be incapable of recognizing the true character of these travellers.

None the less the traveller who is thus abused, knowing that such implacable opposition stems largely from a desire on the part of the builders to defend and protect the priority of their traditions, will seek only to give himself to the truth which, says Jesus, sets men free, and as much as in him lies, live at peace with all men.

So far we have referred to the 'primary' means by which the Wall is constituted. As his powers of observation develop, so the pilgrim becomes aware of secondary, yet none the less powerful aspects of the Wall's substance; material which not only contributes to its basic construction, but also to its regular maintenance and repair. These secondary causes proceed from the pilgrim himself. They have their origins in the conditions and influence to which since childhood, he has been subjected and within which all that makes up his personality has been formed.

From these sources stem what we may call the projected images of God: creatures of the pilgrim's own imagination. Shaped and formed within his consciousness by factors beyond his control, they are projected outwards, as on a cinema screen. From such images, none are entirely free, and to be a traveller in the Way gives no immunity from this inheritance and its consequences. Rather does the pilgrim find opportunity in company with his fellow travellers, to acknowledge this legacy in which all share and to recognize the process by which these images are created. He may then learn how to release them into that Light which can denude them of their power.

The process of creating God-images begins very early in life. With all children deep impressions are formed, primarily by the attitudes and behaviour patterns which prevail in the situations in which they grow up. It is the qualities, positive or otherwise, associated with the adults around them, which for the child quickly become identified with authority. When, in the context of a religious upbringing ultimate authority is related to a God-image, this very image is soon invested with these same characteristics. Thus they become – whatever their nature – God qualities and this process is by no means halted by the verbal injections of what may be regarded as a theologically correct training. For it is not by words that images of God are created or demolished in the unconscious. Indeed what is mistakenly called thorough and systematic religious education, when at variance with emotionally charged God-images, may well become the means of building up deep inner tensions. For this creates a thinking pattern quite at odds with the currents of deep feeling.

An example of this division is frequently found when a teacher indescriminately presents the Father-image of God. To the child whose relationship with its father is one of deep security and love this may be excellent but, for those where the relationship is less than complete or ideal, not only does this image fail to achieve the desired end, it gives God the face of an unacceptable Father. Thus, a God with Father's face is brought to birth. At best this caricature is consciously rejected. It may, however, be pushed below the level of conscious memory thought to be forgotten, but in fact repressed; a wound festering below the surface giving birth to fearful caricatures of the Divine countenance.

By such means is the Wall of confusion reinforced and its parts cemented. So a multiplicity of conscious and unconscious images confront and threaten to overwhelm the pilgrim.

The immediate need in the face of this towering obstacle is the creation of a situation that will reveal the Wall's true character and by which the unreal may be distinguished from the real. The process by which this may take place is already in operation. The pilgrim is both consciously and unconsciously drawing on the resources of the inner reality. He is learning to look from the still centre, to observe without emotional involvement. This, as we have seen, means a distancing of himself from the object of observation. It is the 'being still' which gives birth to 'seeing'. In this way the pilgrim learns how not to react. For the essence of reaction is both fear and panic and efforts to demolish the Wall which spring from such negative emotions will but add to its content and structure. All accurate discernment, all truly creative activity, must spring from the still centre. As this is allowed to happen, the true nature of the Wall of Confusion will be disclosed; the spectre will be uncovered as its insubstantial nature becomes clearly apparent to the observing eye. In this Light which lightens every man it will begin to dissolve.

In Dickens's *Christmas Carol*, the miser Scrooge dreams of three encounters with ghosts: those of Christmas past, Christmas present and Christmas still to come. In his dreams, fears of the past and of the future press in upon him. He awakens from his final dream with indescribable relief to face the objective reality of the present with all its potential and opportunity.

This is the nature of that reality to which every true pilgrim is relating. In the midst of spectres impinging upon his consciousness from without and fantasies arising from within he can, with complete confidence, rest in an objective reality of inexhaustible potential and opportunity which has been described in this way: it is non-personal and yet never impersonal. It is unknowable and unknown. Yet it can be better known than anything else is known. It is both without us and within us. It is eternal rest and at the same time intense activity. It is the countenance of the glory of God which, says St Paul, we have seen in the face of Jesus Christ.

And here is a paradox, for this reality or divine indwelling within the heart of man is greater than the heart of man. Indeed it is greater than mankind. It is the divine dynamic operating in history. It permeates all creation. It is a movement of purpose within the whole created order. And it is with this movement that we seek to align ourselves in meditation. There is no introspective selfish preoccupation. For he who journeys inwards is, in the words of Teilhard de Chardin, 'moving to the very heart of the universe'.

MEDITATIONAL EXERCISE

1 Basic exercise

2 Place yourself as before, in imagination at the centre of a tranquil picture. Now focus upon a point of Light within the heart. Allow this Light steadily to grow, its radiances extending throughout the body and beyond. You are now within the Light and surrounded by it. Its source is within you. Be aware of this welling up of Light from within. Focus and as necessary refocus your attention on this inner fountain of Light, Love and Power.

3 Silence

4 Closing words:
   And the Light shines in the darkness and the darkness can never overcome it.

5 Reading:
   The creation waits with eager longing for the revealing of the sons of God; for the creation was subjected to futility, not of its own will but by the will of him who subjected it in hope; because the creation itself will be set free from its

bondage to decay and obtain the glorious liberty of the children of God.

Romans 8: 19–23

6 Invocation

4

The I AM Identity

Those with childhood memories of visits to the seaside may recall the experience of grappling with the mysteries of the once popular seaside entertainment – the telescope. Most seaside resorts had them. They were usually erected at a high point above the sealine. In order to use them effectively it was necessary to go through the process of adjusting height, clearing the lens, putting in the required coin and, finally, focusing in order to get an accurate picture.

Contemplative meditation, as we saw in Chapter two, may be defined as a certain way of looking, the taking of a particular perspective, and if we are to acquire an accurate understanding of life as a whole, first of all to look at ourselves. Already we are practising this. We can therefore now pose the question, What is it we are doing? and, equally important, What is it that we are not doing?

There are, as we have seen, two things to be avoided. Let us look at them carefully. We must not confuse contemplative observation with introspection. They are quite different. The first is to do with observation from a platform of detached non-reflective concentration. The second, introspection, is an emotional involvement with the object of observation, an involvement which precludes objectivity. The former creates space and freedom of action and growth towards maturity. The latter intensifies emotion and contributes to the building up of anxiety.

Another mistake is to confuse observation with mental analysis – that is not only to look at, but to attempt to dissect the object of observation. The conclusions of such an analysis are inevitably superficial, for this constitutes an isolated intellectual exercise, restricted and limited in its comprehension. Certainly it avoids entanglement with the emotions – indeed it ignores them altogether. The tip of the iceberg, so to speak, is carefully examined, and the mass submerged beneath the surface treated as though it did not exist.

To reach the observer platform from which the pilgrim may see things as they really are requires constant practice. Here we encounter a paradox. It is in the ceasing from activity, the standing back and the stepping into stillness, that such movement is made possible.

These are the practices which spring from, and lend impetus to, that 'will' already operating within the pilgrim. It is a will belonging to that reality which he is now constantly touching. Speaking of this Jesus said: 'If a man obeys this will, he shall know the truth of my teaching'. Aligned with this will, the pilgrim is able to move into the place from which self-observation may be put into practice with accuracy and knowledge.

The movement which this involves has two aspects. It is first of all a conscious and deliberate effort. It therefore contains an element above that which is natural to the pilgrim. Secondly it has a spontaneous character. The former gives birth to the latter. The first is a disciplined creation of conditions within which the second may operate. So periods set aside for the practice of contemplation make possible the meditative way of life.

In putting this into effect the pilgrim is likely to find a common hindrance. In close proximity to the observation platform and somewhat overshadowing it is the Tower of Ignorance. Its immediate appearance is similar to that of the observer platform, for it is also constructed as a means of observation. But the similarity is superficial for, whereas the observer platform provides panoramic and unrestricted views, thus enabling the viewer to see with complete accuracy, the Tower of Ignorance is so constructed as to prevent direct vision, the builders having had no knowledge of the laws governing such a task. Furthermore, certain aspects of the building's construction are based upon the assumption that detached observation is neither desirable nor possible.

The Tower is enclosed, having only three windows. These are labelled activity, involvement and anxiety, and it is in this order that they are approached. These windows are close to the ground. Attached to them are heavy shutters which effectively keep out the Light. When one is opened, any possibility of viewing from the others is blocked by these shutters. Access to this Tower is easy for its doors are always open. Many therefore wander in without conscious will or preparation. Those who leave it do so from dissatisfaction and frustration. The pilgrim who is consciously seeking for that vantage point from which he may see things as they really are, will not here be long delayed, for the will already operating in him is the beginning of that 'asking, seeking and knocking' in response to which Jesus promised that there would be a 'receiving, a finding and an opening'.

Reaching the observation platform, the pilgrim finds himself in the place of stillness and expectancy. It is here that a picture will begin to present itself. Hitherto unrecognized aspects of his being will arise within his consciousness and be brought into sharp focus. This will take place, both in consciously creative periods of stillness and in the business of living. Every conceivable state and stage of living will constitute situations within which self-observation will become possible. And here the pilgrim should be aware that this seeing of things as they really are is never completed, for each day and circumstance will hold within it the necessity for renewed seeing. The responsibility of the pilgrim is to create and recreate conditions in which the picture may emerge, so will he awaken to reality and to glimpses of things as they really are. He will be responding to the cry echoed by the Apostle Paul: 'Awake thou that sleepest and arise from the dead and Christ shall give thee Light.'

The primary picture which unfolds to self-observation will put to flight the commonly held illusion that each human being constitutes a single undivided self; for within the observer's field of vision will emerge the picture of the many selves which constitute a single personality. Each of these he will see as appearing to have a life of its own. When invested with emotional content, a particular 'self' will expand and assume proportions giving it for a short time dominance over the other selves. Each vies constantly with the others for pre-eminence. These selves encompass the whole range of appetites and desires common to man.

As he sees all this the observer will begin to put into effect the law of detachment. This is a process of stepping back and, as this is done, the emotional content of these warring selves is released, their powers decreased and their grip lessened. The observer is looking with knowledge, for he knows that these aspects of the personality are usurpers, entrenched within the citadel of his total being, but nevertheless intruders, having no right of residence. Indeed, although they surround and press upon the still centre, they can never enter or capture it, for this is quite beyond their powers.

These false selves will be revealed to the watcher in their true character: as themselves, servants of the ego which, said Jesus, is the usurper of the true Self; and this pseudo-self, however it may manifest, has a hall-mark by which it can be recognized.

In medieval times many stories were told describing how, in the garb of a monk, the devil would appear to tempt and lure those seeking to follow the path of truth. His face would be well hidden by the monk's cowl, his body covered almost to the ground by the religious habit – almost but not quite, for as he turned to go his true identity would be revealed by the small but unhidden detail of the cloven hoof. For the pseudo-self – and this is what the stories are all about – is always revealed by the single identifying factor, the label of 'I want', a want which when unrecognized or consciously conceded may, in a multitude of ways, become a ruthless demand, even for love.

The 'religious' aspect of the dress assumed by the pseudo-self should not startle or disturb the pilgrim, for this is a guise it may delight to wear. Indeed it may blossom and flourish on religious practices, appear impeccably orthodox and be zealous in propagation of the truth. Of this possibility Jesus gave warning. 'There will', he said, 'be those who protest that they have done good works in my name but of whom I shall say at the last, "I never knew you".'

Through the forming of the picture which reveals objective reality the submerged is now coming to the surface, the hidden is being brought into the Light. The discovery of real identity has begun. At the centre of his being the pilgrim is discovering a place of pure self-consciousness. It is here that awareness is being trained to centre.

Without doubt, the emergence of this picture will present a threat to the ego or false self. In the light of this reality its very existence will be threatened. In the face of this the pilgrim will continue to create and recreate the conditions which make the practice of non-emotional regarding and non-reflective observation possible, for he will know that the existence which is threatened is that of the Usurper. He will find his true security extended. In the words of Jesus: 'Whoever cares for his own safety is lost, but if a man will let himself be lost for my sake, he will find his true self.'

Again, the pilgrim will begin to know that the path of pilgrimage which he has undertaken, the journey followed by all People of the Way, is one of laying down one's life in order to find it – a dying, in order that life may come to birth. For there is no alternative path, no other way. This is that which in the life and death of Jesus is perfectly expressed. Here, historically demonstrated, is the truth that until a man finds his true self through the putting to death of the ego he has no real or permanent identity. This to human vanity is unacceptable and intolerable. For this reason St Paul describes it as the 'offence of the Cross'.

Years ago, an elderly friend told the story of a visit he had once made to Egypt. He took the usual tourist excursions to the Pyramids and the Sphinx. He decided to go further and hired an experienced guide. At first the landscape was familiar and the way ahead clear. This however, gradually gave way to nothing but endless and, to the traveller, anonymous sand dunes. Disturbed, he enquired anxiously of the guide, who unhesitatingly replied: 'I am the way'.

It is through the perfect assurance that I AM, the discovery of true Self-consciousness that the straight path is revealed. This is the new birth without which, said Jesus to Nicodemus, 'no man may enter into the kingdom of heaven'.

Nowhere is this Self-realization more powerfully expressed than in the great I AM sayings of Jesus recorded in St John's Gospel. Again and again he speaks the words. They issue always from this point of essential being and perfect Self-consciousness. And it is this I AM which is the Way, the Door, the Light, the Resurrection and the Life. 'There is no other Way', says Jesus, 'by which men may be saved.'

MEDITATIONAL EXERCISE

1 Basic exercise

2 Within the context of the now familiar picture focus your attention within the still centre. With consciousness centred

here gently repeat the words 'I AM'. If this comes naturally the words may also be visualized in the form of Light within the heart. This may continue for several minutes. As words become superfluous, let them gradually give way to awareness of Light welling up from within the still centre. Hold yourself within this inexhaustible source, this fountain of Light. Relax into it, at the same time keeping your consciousness at all times centred in the heart.

3 Silence

4 Closing sentence:
The eye is the lamp of the body. So, if your eye is sound, your whole body will be full of light.

5 Reading:
Jesus said: 'When the Spirit of truth comes he will guide you into all the truth; for he will not speak on his own authority, but whatever he hears he will speak, and he will declare to you the things that are to come. He will glorify me, for he will take what is mine and declare it to you. All that the Father has is mine; therefore I said that he will take what is mine and declare it to you.'

John 16:12–15

6 Invocation

5

Relationships (1)

The pilgrim Way is a way of life and living is to do with relationships. All of us know that most of life's difficulties can be identified as people – other people. For without other people and the difficulties they create, the business of living would be much pleasanter and much easier. In a word, people are the difficulty.

But the difficulty cannot be quite so simply defined and this for two reasons: the first should be obvious and in theory it is, i.e. that we are all other people to someone else. Secondly, there is the problem of loneliness, for without relationships life is incomplete. All of us in some way require other people. At the highest level we need them for growth into maturity and, at the lowest, as props on which to lean. Those who try to dispense with other people frequently resort, consciously or unconsciously, to substituting inanimate objects or animals for human beings.

These are the facts etched clearly into the self-portrait now being unveiled to the pilgrim. And in the act of looking, his awareness of the implications of this will steadily expand. The perceptions which are centred in a true self-consciousness will go far beyond this. Inherent in this growing understanding of oneself will be an evolution of insight into the nature of man. . The perspectives being created are those which will penetrate the very heart of the human condition. Understanding of the individual will be related to humanity as a whole.

Such perceptions will inevitably involve moving into an area which, to the advancing pilgrim, will appear to be one of great darkness. The darkness is that of an immense shadow falling across the straight path. Its shape and size he will not at first perceive. He will be conscious only of its intensity. This is the shadow cast by the great Prison House of Humanity, for the pilgrim has come face to face with the human predicament – the nature of man. It is to the facing of this that the path of experimental wisdom must inevitably lead.

The pilgrim is touching within himself the psyche of all humanity. He is awakening to the truth that man, by the fact of his existence, constitution and conditioning is caught up with all creation upon the great wheel of eternal recurrence. Man is of the earth earthy. From this he has taken form and to it, as by its gravitational pull, he must inevitably return. The whole creation is involved in this perpetual cycle of birth, death and rebirth. It is within this inexorable law that both the anguish and hope of mankind exist. This the pilgrim has already uncovered within himself and it is through this self-discovering that he is enabled to plumb the depths of manhood and its hidden mysteries.

On the periphery of the shadow there appears a large and man-made structure. This is in the nature of a scaffolding. Upon it are stationed a great many people. Each one is engaged in intense activity, but this takes place within the confines of the space he occupies. All are seated and none moves from his place. The activities with which these workers are so preoccupied cover a wide range of skills. Writers, artists and craftsmen of many kinds apply themselves with great assiduousness to the task on hand. All are giving themselves to the work of taking the measurements of the shadow. Few amongst them have any awareness of their companions, for each is dedicated exclusively to the skills of his own craft. The overwhelming involvement of each is with that portion of the shadow best seen from the position he occupies upon the scaffolding and most suited to his particular capabilities. One thing they have in common. None, however skilled in his particular field, is able from the scaffolding, properly to comprehend the shadow's shape or substance. The totality, both of the human predicament and its potential, eludes them.

These are they, worthy of respect, who though limited and partial in their comprehension, nevertheless acknowledge the existence of the shadow. They are the skilled representatives of science, philosophy, psychology and religion who since the dawning of human self-consciousness have wrestled, each in his own way, with the problem now confronting the pilgrim. Their terms of reference do not include that by which the pilgrim travels – i.e. that truth is that which in a given situation awakens man to reality.

The pilgrim too, like all the People of the Way, understands as yet but in part, yet because of the assurance born of walking in the Way and the knowledge reflected in the still, clear pool of reflection, he continues to walk straight ahead. His confidence is rooted in that which hitherto has guided his every step, and faith gives access to further knowledge. He knows that if he would see more and advance further the darkness cannot be avoided. It must be faced and entered. It is as he does this that its true nature begins to unfold. The extent of the darkness is beyond his capacity to measure, yet because he is looking with the eyes of the heart he is able to penetrate its substance. Although its outline is inconstant it has a basic shape. Its form is that of a man. He looks steadfastly without fear. As he does so, he understands that within this one man all mankind exists. Here the whole of humanity is gathered into one and all its parts are focused.

The composition of the darkness is of many parts and particles, yet in its essential nature one and uniform. The destiny of all humanity is woven into its fabric. The substance holds the elements of suffering and death, and with all its parts the pilgrim now identifies. Nevertheless, he moves on, unafraid. The darkness has no power to overwhelm him or to eclipse his vision. The reason for this will become apparent when his passage through the shadow is completed. His progress now is prompted by the knowledge of what has gone before and hope in all that lies ahead. He is entering fully into the mystery of the earth-born man described by St Paul as the first man, Adam. He knows himself also to be caught up in that plan and purpose by which alone humanity can fulfil its destiny.

Through penetrating the shadow, the pilgrim's perceptions are sharpened and his vision enlarged. The very act of faith required for entering in has effected also an entrance for the light. He finds himself surrounded by this light and by its illumination the interior becomes visible.

He discerns its magnitude, its shape and size, and discovers himself to be within a vast model of a man – a figure whose essential being is now revealed. At the same time he is aware of the presence of another group of people. Unlike those outside the shadow, these are constantly moving around, examining the contours of the interior. In their hands they have instruments by which they are busily engaged in taking measurements. The results of these they record in the form of blueprints, which are bound together so as to provide maps for the People of the Way. These are the architects of the hidden sciences whose origins are chiefly in the East. Their access to the shadow's interior was by another and secret way. Because of this their labours are conducted without the benefit of the light which accompanies all those who enter by the straight path. For this reason they are unable to perceive that the contours of the shadow are ever changing and therefore beyond the scope of those instruments by which they measure.

In the face of this intense activity the pilgrim will become aware of his need once more to step back, and to be still. In so doing he will keep his equilibrium and, whilst recognizing the skills of the draftsmen about him, will know of a certainty that only in following the straight path can he maintain a vision of the whole.

In renewing his perspectives he begins to recognize the primary source from which the shadow takes its substance and by which it is perpetuated. The origin of this is an increasing torrent of emotional energy, uncontrolled and undirected. These constitute the forces by which the great mass of humanity operates. They are the manifestation within man of the laws of repelling and attracting. Human likes, dislikes, attachments and aversions are seen to operate quite independently of will and intention. They are entirely reactional. These are largely ungoverned and ungovernable aspects of human nature. In unbroken stream they both pour into and issue forth from the substance of the shadow. Such activity is instinctual, an automatic functioning of that part of man he holds in common with the animal kingdom. In part its manifestation is regulated by legal sanctions, ethical structures and religious ideals, imposed by society upon itself for preservation, stability and advancement. The effects of these are what is commonly called civilization. By this means much of the energy thus created is channelled and directed. The residue is the substance of universal wars.

The pilgrim will also observe a second source from which the shadow takes its substance. This is a moving force of very great intensity. Its elements are those which constitute power. They are combined reserves of intellect and will. Its fruit is calculated and frequently ruthless activity.

The reason for this is that the human activity to which it gives birth is under the control of the pseudo-self. Its movements are therefore subject to the multiplicity of 'I's'. It is ultimately self-seeking and destructive of humanity.

The force of reactionary emotions will frequently stimulate this second level of human activity. This in turn generates further instinctual energies. So is the shadow re-created and renewed. These two sources are those by which the greater part of human behaviour patterns are formed.

All this the pilgrim sees as contributing to the form and

shape of the man of the earth. This act of fearless seeing will enable him to pass through the darkness to the further side of the shadow. And here he will emerge into a place of very great light. Its radiance is like that of the sun. Yet it emanates from the very substance of the shadow itself. Viewed from where he now stands, every particle of darkness which constitutes the man is seen to contain within itself a seed of brilliant light by which a process of transformation is taking place. The man of darkness is being changed. Its shape is assuming constancy of form and unity in all its parts. A great being of light is emerging from the shadow. This evolution of the shadow's substance is the result of a third and mysterious level of activity. The source of this the pilgrim cannot see. Yet of its existence he has no doubt. This hidden work is beautifully described in Bunyan's *Pilgrim's Progress*:

> I saw in my dream a place where was a fire burning against a wall. . . and he had about him to the backside of the wall where he saw a man with a vessel of oil in his hand of which he did continually cast (but secretly) into the fire. Then said Christian: 'What means this?' The interpreter answered: 'This is Christ who continually with the oil of His grace maintains the work already begun in the heart. . . and in that thou sawest that the man stood behind the wall to maintain the fire that is to teach thee that it is hard to see how this work is maintained.'

This is that very work by which the energies of instinct, intellect and will are being transmuted. It is effected by a third and superhuman level of activity. By this means does the dying man evolve into what St Paul calls 'the man from Heaven, the second Adam'. The operation of this level has an infallible authentication. It is proved by the manifestation of light. And this light itself has many parts. They are described in the New Testament as love, joy, longsuffering, gentleness, meekness, temperance, faith.

Through his recognition of this level of operation the pilgrim himself becomes part of its activity. He provides a means by which this third force enters the human condition. He thus makes possible a great downpouring of the light of which he himself becomes a transmitter. These vibrant and powerful energies thus become a cross – the cross of death and resurrection is established in individual and within corporate man. Relationships are transformed and other people, who at the level of reaction and power appear as unfailingly difficult, are seen to have value and significance in themselves, and to be an integral part of 'everyman' in the process of transformation.

This is the work of lifting humanity from the levels of reaction and selfish interest. It is the raising of human consciousness to the level of the heart, and the means by which men become co-workers with God. It is described by St Paul in the imagery of a three-dimensional universe. This universe is within men. 'If you then be risen with Christ,' he writes, 'seek those things which are above, where Christ sitteth on the right hand of God.'

MEDITATIONAL EXERCISE

1 Basic exercise

2 Place yourself as before within a tranquil picture. Within this context become aware of a downpouring of Light. Hold yourself within this movement, allowing it to pour down through the crown of the head. Let your consciousness follow the Light's movement – crown, forehead, throat, chest and down into the earth.
From the centre of your being, the heart, allow the Light to radiate outwards, so forming a cross of Light, the centre of which is your centre. Hold yourself in this manner, as a channel of the Light.

3 Silence

4 Closing sentence:
Jesus said: 'I am the Light of the world: he that followeth me shall not walk in darkness, but shall have the light of Life.'

5 Reading:
Jesus said: 'And I, when I am lifted up from the earth, will draw all men to myself.' He said this to show by what death he was to die. The crowd answered him, 'We have heard from the law that the Christ remains for ever. How can you say that the Son of Man must be lifted up? Who is this Son of Man?' Jesus said to them, 'The light is with you for a little longer. Walk while you have the light, lest the darkness overtake you; He who walks in the darkness does not know where he goes. While you have the light, believe in the light, that you may become sons of light.'

John 12:32–36

6 Invocation

6

Relationships (2)

In Lewis Carroll's *Through the Looking Glass* Alice is seen at a certain stage of her adventure running hard in order to remain in one place. As the pilgrim grows in self-awareness he will recognize this to be true in regard to many of his relationships. An enormous amount of nervous energy is expended in maintaining the status quo.

Many day-to-day relationships bear on the surface the apparent marks of harmony and compatibility. These are often superficial and disguise the real situation. Beneath the surface is a discord destructive to all concerned. These relationships contain and foster – often on the level of the unconscious – the whole range of negative emotions from mild antipathy to intense animosity. Hidden beneath the mask of that amiability required by convention or self-seeking, they constitute the real level of human interaction. This is the source of much emotional and mental pressure and the cause of many diseases.

The journey so far has taught the pilgrim that the validity of the path he follows is measured, not by the accumulation of information but by its application in living. The practice of meditation and techniques of contemplation have value and significance only in so far as they increase the capacity for overcoming difficult circumstances and relating to people who are felt to be difficult. This is at the centre of the pilgrim's consciousness, for by his committal to the straight path he has added knowledge to faith. This is now to be used in establishing foundations for the building of right relationships.

Here the pilgrim finds himself at a point of intersection in the Way. He has arrived at a place where many paths converge and a large crowd is assembled. At the point of convergence is an island in the form of a roundabout. At first sight the crowd seems to consist of fellow travellers and people of the Way. Each one greets the pilgrim, applauds his dedication to self-knowledge and assures him that they also are committed to exploring the realms of the subconscious. Each one extols with enthusiasm the virtues of the path by which he has come to the roundabout. All show signs of great restlessness. They move at varying speeds but all in one direction. The pilgrim perceives that this movement is a circular one which takes them as by perpetual motion around the central island – a place which, for each one, holds great fascination. Their preoccupation is with this central point and to it they all are gravitating. Because of this they fail to see the signpost directing travellers to the straight path. Many of their number have already gathered on the island where they are now seated. Each one is totally preoccupied with himself and all have lost sight of the path ahead which now rises sharply to higher ground. To those seated on the island their self-exploration has become an end in itself, the journey to higher ground is forgotten.

The habit of regular observation now stands the pilgrim in good stead. He sees the signpost and moves ahead to the next stage of the journey. He has acquired understanding of the necessity to reach a new level of opera-tion. This is his goal, for he recognizes that by this alone can relationships be changed and the human dilemma transformed. Freeing himself by this means from the mag-netic attraction of the island, he sets his face towards higher ground. Here he finds that the very will to do this is the act of climbing and he discovers himself at once to be at the place he is seeking. When he has reached the top of the hill, his first discovery is that of a new vantage-point and he is immediately aware of something which until now, has been totally hidden from him. In a manner not previously experienced, he knows himself to be surrounded by people. These press in on every side, yet he feels no pressure from their presence; therefore he does not recognize that these are they whom hitherto he has equated with the word 'problem'; the ones he has dismissed as of no consequence. The reason for this is that a very great change has begun to take place at the level of the subconscious. This change is within the pil-grim himself. The results are the birth of a new capacity for seeing other people. In the eyes of the ones within whom this transformation is happening it is the other people who appear to have changed, for in his eyes they are assuming a new and changed appearance. This has been brought about by the ascent to higher ground – to ground which is fully open to the Light streaming down from above. It is as though scales have fallen from the pilgrim's eyes and new dimensions of humanity are re-vealed. The hidden splendour which he has begun to realize and release within himself is now unveiled to others. The once despised and rejected are seen each to have substance and potential.

To see in this way is the first step in the creation of a new level of human interaction. Yet as we have seen, the beginnings of this change are primarily in the area of the subconscious, for the higher ground is reached not by thought but through fidelity to the vision unfolding from within. So does the pilgrim reach the level of human activity where, by the operation of a third force, new attitudes to people are fashioned. At the precise nature of this force, we shall look later.

Equally unaware, at the level of thought as to what is happening, are those who until now have constituted nothing more than 'difficulties' in the pilgrim's way. No longer are they objects to be changed or removed by the will of another, for they have been given place, space and cognizance. Imperceptibly, they begin to feel accepted, a channel for healing is now opened and into this the third force flows. The transformation of relationships has begun.

As the pilgrim becomes accustomed to the place he occupies upon the higher ground, so will he begin to understand the energies generated at this level of activity and which together constitute the substance of the third force. Will and desire are now combining within him to co-operate with this transforming power, and as this happens there is born in him a new sense of responsibility. What he is now relating to through his new-found understanding of other people is the universal plan for mankind. Those who once appeared as hindrances to his own unfoldment are known to be part of that very pilgrimage to which he is committed. Everyone has a part in the new creation being wrought from the substance of the shadow man.

To further this new creation is now his overriding concern. To do so means conscious co-operation with the newly-discovered source of creative energy, for through this alone can the healing of the nations be brought about. This is the vision afforded by the higher ground, as it is here that the energies which shape the destiny of man are generated. Yet if the pilgrim is to fulfil the vision and harness these resources, he must move on.

From the plateau the path dips sharply down. The Way, though steep, is still very straight. It leads directly into the Valley of Service, and here the pilgrim is presented with a choice. At the place where the path leaves the high ground and to the lefthand side, stands a building of great beauty. The house is large and securely built, having foundations that go deep into the soil. It is enclosed by five walls, the proportions of which are very satisfying. This is the House of the Senses. Writ large above the entrance are words offering security of tenure to all who desire to take up residence. A second but smaller sign promises ample opportunity for the employment of time and energy to all comers. The ground upon which the pilgrim is standing commands both a view of the house and the descending pathway, though the shape of the house prevents him from seeing clearly into the valley. Each step towards the house impairs his view of what lies below, and from the gateway to the house the valley appears to be filled only with black cloud.

It is only as the pilgrim returns his attention to the path itself and focuses his gaze directly into the valley that an incentive to continue the journey is renewed. As he does so, the clouds below begin to disperse and he finds again the will and desire to descend. With the disappearance of the cloud the contents of the valley are clearly visible. Its floor is covered with a vast company of people. There is about them a great stillness or lack of movement, for all are suffering handicaps and disabilities – emotional, mental and physical. Some of these are of the most distressing kind, having no means of alleviation or healing. As he descends yet further into the valley and the distance from the House of the Senses increases, so is he again aware of a change in people: a transformation is taking place in the appearance of those towards whom he is moving. Each one is seen to be diffused in the Light within which, whatever the nature of his need and however distressing his condition, he finds comfort and healing.

The threads by which the pilgrim feels himself to be drawn now take tangible form. Their substance also is that of Light, for like is now calling to like. What the pilgrim does not see – for his attention is given wholly to the people whose dwelling-place he is now entering – is that the golden threads are the very means by which the healing Light is reaching them. Its source is the plateau, and the pilgrim the means by which it reaches the people. So he passes through them and, as he does so, ministers to their need. And drawn by the pilgrim's threads of Light many free themselves from the torpor of the valley and move into the straight path. For the Love of God, which is the nature of the third force, has been shed abroad in their hearts.

MEDITATIONAL EXERCISES

1 Basic exercise

2 From within the picture become aware again of the Light
within the heart, aware also that the Light within one is the
Light within all the people of the Way throughout the world.
See yourself linked at the level of the heart in a vast network
of Light encircling the globe. Along the golden threads that
go from heart to heart, peace, love and power are given and
received.

3 Silence

4 Closing sentence:
'If we walk in the light as he is in the light, we have
fellowship with one another.'

5 Reading:
By this we know love, that he laid down his life for us:
and we ought to lay down our lives for the brethren. But
if any one has the world's goods and sees his brother in
need, yet closes his heart against him, how does God's
love abide in him? Little children, let us not love in word
or speech but in deed and in truth. By this we shall know
that we are of the truth, and reassure our hearts before
him.

1 John 3:16–19

6 Invocation

7

The Mystic In Society

The Mystic is both a child of his time and a universal man. He belongs to the age into which he is born, yet he cannot be confined within its limited horizons or swamped by its transitory preoccupations. The perceptions being formed by his personal disciplines have a significance beyond that of his own transformation. His capacity for detached observation will increasingly throw light on the needs of contemporary society. He stands apart in order that he may properly identify with his contemporaries.

By the nature of the path he follows, it is impossible for the pilgrim to be concerned only with his own spiritual evolution, and to exist as an isolated island of tranquillity in a troubled world. This for him is a contradiction in terms. The consciousness fostered by experimental wisdom is not that of a private pietism, an opting out of life's realities, but of a universal self operating within the great mass of humanity. The dynamic he is uncovering within himself is struggling to come to birth within all mankind. His concern therefore is with wholeness of living and with life as a whole, the cultivation of a universal consciousness.

In the light of this holistic vision, which is of the essence of a true mysticism, the pilgrim's path unfolds.

Times set aside for meditation are but periods for the conscious cultivation of an impulse at all times present and the practice of a presence which is all-pervading. The undeviating purpose of this, whether by individuals or groups, is for the steady raising of sights and the widening of horizons. Such systematic focusing will prevent those meeting in groups from a preoccupation with one another and individuals from profitless speculation about self-improvement. Rather will they find themselves drawn increasingly into attitudes of reverential awareness, a consciousness of being in the presence of a dynamic which prompts the great movements of history and shapes the destiny of men.

It is the uncovering of this dynamic within their own span of history for which the people of the Way have a special responsibility and for which contemplative living gives a particular insight. From perspectives taken outside of time, i.e. from the still centre, the pilgrim understands the meaning of time. He is a conscious link between time and eternity, the transitory and that which is unchanging. In his *Four Quartets* (Faber) T. S. Eliot describes this as the still point of the turning world where past and future are gathered. Here man may stand beyond time and its limitations in order to learn its true significance. This is the threshold where he must stand if he is to understand and transmit all that pertains to wholeness for the individual and for society. It is the only valid source of vision.

In the Jewish Scriptures frequent use is made of the imagery of the watchman. His function was to patrol the walls of the enclosed city. From the ramparts he held a commanding view of all that was taking place. He alone in the city had a picture of the whole. From sunset until dawn the cry would echo periodically from within the confines of the city: 'Watchman, what of the night?' For the watchman stood in the place from where an accurate report could be transmitted.

A nation's safety, it has been said, depends on the number of its contemplatives. They are the watchmen in any society. They alone occupy a vantage-point between and above separated communal interests. The universal plan and purpose to which they are committed transcends all divisions. It can never be encapsulated within exclusive groupings whether religious, political or social. Of these divisions and their superficial nature the contemplative must be acutely aware. At the same time he will perceive the superficial nature of the wall which, at the level of thought and ideology, perpetuates such groupings. The very word 'pilgrim' implies movement and the movement prompted from the still point of the turning world will ever free the contemplative to be truly a pilgrim, and to move easily across all barriers.

This is the freedom which authenticates the people of the Way. Thus do they stand as powerful reconcilers at points of intersection in a divided world. In their refusal to give cognizance to separativeness they are able to penetrate all barriers. This is the operation of that very spirit by which Jesus of Nazareth refused to recognize all man-made divisions. His ministry transcended the boundaries erected by belief systems whether national, political or religious. This is symbolized by the statement in the Epistle to the Hebrews that 'he has broken down the middle wall of partition between Jew and Gentile'.

The level of consciousness which makes intersection possible and from which the holistic vision may be renewed and transmitted is described by Happold in *Religious Faith and Twentieth-Century Man* (Darton, Longman and Todd 1980), p. 163:

> It would be misleading to think of Intersection as a purely intellectual process, as an effort to reconcile conflicting concepts solely at the level of intellect. Rather a union of spiritual intuition and rational thought is brought into play, so that, though the intellect is not asleep, indeed it is very active, it ceases to be the only instrument of knowing. The whole act of knowing is carried out at a higher level in which what before appeared as contradictories are spontaneously unified and reconciled.

Happold also describes one whom he regards as 'one of the remarkable and representative figures of our time who in her own life exemplified the power of a ministry of intersection'.

> Through the profound mystical experience which she describes (Simone Weil) . . . . was drawn to Christ. She, however, refused to be baptized into the Catholic Church, because she felt that Christianity, while Catholic by right, was not so in fact. It was not a truly incarnated Christianity; too much was outside it . . . . she wrote . . . . 'I should betray the truth, that is the aspect of truth which I see, if I left the point where I have been since my birth, at *the intersection of Christianity and everything that is not Christian*.' p. 160.

The path which brings the pilgrim to an awareness of the great opportunities of service to mankind offered by intersection leads also and at once to an alternative possibility. For as he ponders on this, he sees a sign inviting him in a direction parallel to but at a level lower than the straight path. It points towards a large pavilion described as the Library of Truth.

As he enters the building, the pilgrim's eye is at once drawn to the walls. From ceiling to floor they are covered with colourfully presented sacred texts. Arranged against the walls are many banners. These also display quotations from the Scriptures. At the same time his ears are assailed by a deafening noise. He quickly detects its origins; it is caused by the excited and agitated conversations of a great number of groups engaged in the study of large and ancient volumes. All the members of the groups are either reading aloud or quoting to their fellows. The students vie with one another in drawing attention to their favourite texts, and are frantically searching the Scriptures to find the truth. Almost all are speaking. Those who are prevented from doing so are but awaiting their own opportunity. The rapid turning over of many pages adds to the cacophony of sound.

As he passes through the building, representatives from every group gather around the pilgrim and press literature upon him. Although this is done with courtesy and charm, the number and volume of the books they offer is such as would constitute a burden grievous to be born. He now observes a steady stream of students who, having completed the studies offered by the groups, are taking banners from the walls and moving towards the exit. Holding them aloft, their lips moving in constant repetition of all that they have learned, they leave the pavilion still travelling along a track parallel to the straight path.

Reaching the exit the pilgrim now recognizes that he

has passed through the School of Contradictions. Stepping carefully back and distancing himself from the noise, he turns and looks again at the texts upon the walls. Their appearance is now changing. The vast array of Biblical fragments are coming together as parts of a whole. The multitude of words assumes a unity of shape. No longer static, their colours move together in harmonious blending. They form a picture of which the pilgrim and the path are both a part. From within this harmony of movement, shape and colour the pilgrim's eye is brought again to focus on the way ahead. And by moving again into the straight path he knows 'the truth' which Jesus said would surely set men free; truth which can never exist in static form or be imprisoned in sacred words. For it is in following in the Way that man may know the truth, i.e. awaken to reality.

From the School of Contradictions the two paths continue side by side – the lower followed by its students carrying banners and now appearing like crusaders, the higher by the pilgrim. Both paths lead quickly into low-lying ground. On both sides of the lower path the waves of a turbulent swamp break angrily, threatening to engulf it. The motion of the waters is caused by the flow of many streams converging on the swamp. Here the crusaders stake their banners by the water's edge, where many more are already planted. They quickly join a company of labourers who, on either side of the path and some distance into the swamp, are already struggling to reverse the flow of the waves. Great urgency inspires the work, and the agitation of the swamp caused by their efforts matches the turbulence of the waves. It is clear that their work is unsuccessful, and this for two reasons. The frenzy of their activities increases the erosion of the lower pathway, and the dams they are building, being constructed of the very substance of the swamp, quickly collapse.

The labourers are warriors for the truth who battle valiantly against the erosion of standards in society. Nobly motivated, they fail to see that energy so directed does but generate those very forces they seek to overcome. Such activity is self-defeating.

From the level at which the pilgrim is now travelling he commands in all directions vistas of unparalleled splendour and very great diversity; the beauty of towns and cities, of wide spaces and vast crowds, scenes of sorrow mingling with joy, despair and hope. All this unfolds before him. Nevertheless he sees enough to discern the emerging of a universal pattern of purpose and of hope. The straight path stretches far ahead and into infinity. He sees that there is still a very great distance to travel, and that there can be no respite from his moving forward. Yet does he also know that where he now stands upon the straight path is the best of all places in which to be.

MEDITATIONAL EXERCISE

1 Basic exercise

2 Extend your concept of a tranquil picture to the whole world. You may in imagination visualize this as a great orb of Light. Allow this gradually to build up before you. Then as it were step into the picture and place yourself at its centre. Become aware of Love and Peace which are of the essence of this

Light. Let it radiate from your own heart, flowing out in compassion to the whole world.

3 Silence

4 Closing sentence:
   You are the light of the world. A city set on a hill cannot be hid.

5 Reading:
   See what love the Father has given us, that we should be called children of God; and so we are. . . . Beloved we are God's children now; it does not yet appear what we shall be, but we know that when he appears we shall be like him, for we shall see him as he is. And every one who thus hopes in him purifies himself as he is pure.

1 John 3:1–3

6 Invocation

Epilogue: The Mystic's Vision

It is a characteristic of the age in which we live that, in spite of the forces of separativeness working in society, it is increasingly difficult for men to live in boxes – religious or secular – whether such boxes be created by patterns of thought or modes of living. The day when any group of people could, without too much difficulty, adhere to a way of life or set pattern of beliefs and preserve them against erosion from within, or irresistible pressure from without, is rapidly passing. Anyone who has reached middle life can look back and see within the limits of their own experience, this process of erosion and pressure.

That this is a universal phenomenon is now apparent. The world is shrinking fast in the sense that on every level of happening and experience little of significance can escape universal notice. As a corollary to this, since World War I there has been increased awareness of the need to bring the nations of the world together in some kind of co-operation, if for no other reason than the need to survive.

On the political level there are now, broadly speaking, three major world groupings of the nations: the Western nations, the Eastern block and the Third World. Such groupings are in many ways artificial. They have been brought into being by pressure from without rather than natural movements from within and, in spite of their political frameworks and economic substructures, they are superficial, being in most cases unrelated to those factors which create real cohesiveness within society. Ethnic, cultural and religious divisions, although at present subservient to these imposed structures, represent greater and more powerful forces. At a deeper level still, which we shall examine later, there are factors which really determine the unity of the nations. Nevertheless, the present groupings are an indication of worldwide concern that without some kind of unity amongst the nations there can be no hope of a future for the world.

Let us look a little more closely at how this universal consciousness is revealing and seeking to express itself in the 'worlds' in which we live and move and have our being, and in which pilgrimage must be pursued. The polarization of politics in Britain between left and right is but the reflection of a world polarization. It is the political and global phenomenon of our age and it is a necessary process, for it presents the opportunity and possibility of human evolution and growth. There is no inevitability about this. The destiny of man in the short term or time term as distinct from eternity is within his own hands and responsibility.

What could emerge – and indeed is already emerging, is a realization that there is not one grouping, one corpus of political dogma and, most important of all, one individual leader, by which, or from whom, a solution can be found to the human dilemma of how to avoid self-destruction and promote a future. That this perception is growing is good, but its emergence is of itself not sufficient, for unless it is informed by, and consciously linked to, that very dimension from which it takes its authentic impulse, it will inevitably founder on anxiety generated by frustration and will end in despair. This, too, we are already witnessing. There are many movements of a potentially violent nature endeavouring to deal with the situation. Sadly, these are often instigated by groups and individuals who hāve a passionate concern for the well-being of their fellow men. Their vision is of a unified mankind, but this is frequently no more than idealism, for its human energy has not been consciously linked to that spiritual impulse without which it must inevitably turn in upon itself and generate further discord and disharmony.

There is today a great profusion of noble sentiments and high ideals. Mankind has for centuries been capable of generating such ideals and sentiments – as witness, for two thousand years the role of the Christian Church, which has consistently propagated the notion of love for God and man. The pressure of a shrinking world and increasing threat of global destruction has produced a new proliferation and expression of these ideas and a sense of urgency in making them known. But divorced from what we may call the supra-human dimension, mankind is quite incapable of realizing these ideals within itself, and so neutralizing the negative forces which dominate society today. The propagators of high ideals themselves become instruments of that very disintegration they desire so much to avert. They generate anxiety and this in turn breeds violence and reaction.

It is easy for us to see this process working out in the

political arena, but the contradiction between idealism and reality is apparent in other areas of life. It permeates all areas of humanitarian and religious concern. Some aspects of this are being faced by the Roman Catholic Church where, in South America, priests with the highest possible motives align themselves with violent currents of reaction against social injustices. Their aims are high, their vision impeccable, but often it is the currents of reaction which eventually submerge the Christian idealists, for their own understanding of, and alignment with, the spiritual dimension is less than adequate for the situation. The urgent need for the people of the Way is the power of discernment.

In Britain, since the fifties, there has been a great wave of feeling against many of the patent hypocrisies, injustices and self-exploitation within society, and new and high ideals have been projected and instilled into our thinking. What has been called 'New Age Consciousness' has, in less than twenty years, brought about a revolution in thought over such things as human relationships, the interaction of the human, animal, vegetable and mineral kingdoms, and the destiny of man.

There has been a pinpointing of human responsibilities; but here also the contradiction is still apparent. Idealism, albeit now of a cosmic kind, has generally outpaced alignment with those very forces of which the New Age Movement has spoken and is still speaking eloquently. Nevertheless this New Age concept indicates a significant step forward in the evolution of global consciousness, for it has frequently indicated, and occasionally articulated and expressed, that very impulse within the human psyche wherein lies the potential for a significant forward leap in mankind's mastery of himself, and in taking responsible control of his destiny.

This new philosophy has brought into rational thought-form the concept of a holistic understanding where both man and his environment are to be seen as component parts of a whole. Science, religion, medicine, education, the arts, agriculture, politics and economics – every area of life is seen as destined to express this wholeness. Without doubt, it is this impulse which is now seeking to express itself within society.

In the early days of this century there appeared in the West two outstanding men whose insight in this respect enabled them powerfully to touch and discern this dimension. This gave birth to what may be described as an inside view of history: Rudolf Steiner and Teilhard de Chardin were both outstanding seers. An outside view of history invests it with meaning and purpose in rationales and frameworks resulting from the disciplines of rational thought. These may range from the philosophical to the theological. There are many such frameworks from which to choose. To proceed from the inside is different; for this means to establish a perspective which, while mindful of outside views, allies itself with the movement from within. This was the way taken by these two men. Teilhard limited his inner perceptions to proceed no further than appeared to him to be consistent with the theology or outside perspectives of his Church. Steiner had no such problems to contend with. Nevertheless, the self-imposed restrictions of Teilhard prevented further crystallization of the dynamic which he tapped and released, into a new static form; whereas Rudolf Steiner's apparent freedom eventually gave birth to an alternative system which could incur the danger of repeating the process of encapsulating its own dynamic. They indicated and uncovered a dynamic within the whole created order: an evolution of consciousness, a movement of convergence towards fulfilment and the consummation of history.

It is in full and conscious co-operation with this movement that the people of the Way must move if they are to understand and interpret to their generation the inside meaning of history. In so doing they become part of the dynamic of convergence which leads to what Teilhard de Chardin calls (every mystic's dream) – described by St Paul as 'the time when God is all and in all'.

Appendix

Meditation: An Explanation

The word meditation has a variety of usages and meanings. As used in this book it refers always and simply to discovering a point of consciousness within oneself beyond the process of thought and the tides of emotion.

The purpose of such meditation is union with the Source – or God. Certain simple techniques directed towards the control of body, mind and emotions have by long tradition both in East and West established themselves as useful towards the achievement of this aim.

They should be seen and used always as a means to an end and never as an end in themselves. In pursuit of this aim they may eventually drop away or be discarded, the guidelines which they established having become part of a whole way of life. The aim towards which they are directed is constant and unchanging.

To achieve this, interior stillness is necessary. The techniques used therefore are concerned with effecting a measure of freedom from the distractions of emotions and intellect.

This does not mean suppression of these two aspects of our being, but rather a recognition that they are but part of the whole, and that if they are to constitute a harmonious part they must be trained to relate to another dimension. This third area of our being is referred to as 'the still centre'. It is 'still' because it constitutes a point of consciousness free from the perturbations of emotions and thoughts. Yet is it also a source of activity. This activity is beyond sense perception. When put into operation it brings will, intellect and emotion into a harmonious working relationship. These may be regarded as the essential ingredients for fully creative living.

BASIC MEDITATIONAL EXERCISE

Intention

The intention of each exercise is to discover and relate to the still centre within, that is the heart. It may therefore be described as Christ-centred. These exercises may be used by individuals or groups.

Steps to Take
The Body

The first step concerns the physical body. Our aim is to find a position which combines relaxation and alertness. For most people this means sitting in a straight-backed chair. The head should be held erect, the hands clasped loosely in the lap or placed palms flat against the thighs, and the feet against the floor or tucked beneath the chair. This position will be modified according to individual needs. What is important is that as far as possible the position of the body should express the intention of the meditator. The physical form so becomes an outward sign of an inner state of being, that is of relaxed alertness.

The Breath

The body is now in position and we are ready to follow a process of relaxation. It is helpful to relate this to the breathing. This is done systematically. Begin with the head and on the outbreath relax the scalp and facial muscles. Do the same with the shoulders, arms, waist, thighs, legs and feet. Finally breathe out several times as though through all the pores of the body, consciously relaxing the whole physical frame. If you become aware of the tightening up of any muscles, return to that part and again consciously relax. Take this slowly.

Observation

With the mind's eye now observe your body – relaxed yet alert. Reverence your body, that is, accept it as a unique God-given vehicle of the real you.

The Emotions

Allow yourself to become aware of your emotions. They too constitute a body. Unlike the physical body it is not confined in one limited space. It is immensely 'busy' in many areas. Allow yourself to become aware of any areas of emotional tension. Do not try to deal with or repress them. Recognize them; observe, acknowledge and let them go. As with the physical body, the process of stepping back from emotional tension may be related to the breathing, so on each outbreath we let go of the pressures and the tensions.

The Intellect

The uncontrolled activity of the intellect blocks off true awareness. As with the emotions, so with the intellect, we need to distance ourselves, to step back from the incessant chatter of the brain. To 'try' to do this can be self-defeating. Allow the mind gradually to quieten down. Gently allow it to relate to one thing. So gradually bring the attention to the centre of the chest and allow it to focus there.

The Still Centre

We are now identifying the heart of our being. This is the still centre, the place of 'perfect clear perception'.

Refocusing

If and when the attention wanders, as you become aware of this, so gently return to the focal point and centre again. Remember it is the 'intention' that matters. Each return to the centre reinforces this.

Visualization

The concept of light is basic to each of the seven exercises. This Light has the qualities both of peace and love. It is that described in the New Testament as the Light of the World.

This exercise may occupy from five to fifteen minutes and forms the basis for each meditational exercise.

Two points to remember

1. The Light is always present within the heart.

2. Centred in this Light, you are always in complete control.

Closing Invocation

May the Light that shows the Way illuminate the mind,
May the Love that knows the Truth unfold within the heart,
May the Power that gives true Life arise within the soul,
Let Light and Love and Power raise all in Christ to God.

Omega Invocation